"Whoever fasts Ramadan with imaan
and the hope of reward
will be forgiven his previous sins."

IBN MAJAH

Beautiful Du'as Of The Prophet ﷺ

ALLAHUMMAR ZUQNI ḤUBBUKA, WA ḤUBBA MAN YANFA`UNI ḤUBBUHU `INDAK. ALLAHUMMA MA RAZAQTANI MIMMA UḤIBBU FAJ'ALHU QUWWATAN LI FIMA TUḤIBB. ALLAHUMMA WA MA ZAWAITA `ANNI MIMMA UḤIBBU FAJ'ALHU FARAGHAN LI FIMA TUḤIBB).
O Allah grant me Your love and the love of those whose love will benefit me with You. O Allah, whatever you have provided me of that which I love, then make it strength for me for that which You love. O Allah, and what you have kept from me of that which I love, then make it for me a period of rest in that which You love. (Tirmidhi)

ALLAHUMMA ATINA FI DUNYA HASANATAN WA FIL AKHIRATI HASANATAN WA QINA 'ADHABA ANNAR.
O Allah, grant us the good in this world and the good in the Hereafter and save us from the torment of Hell-Fire. (Muslim)

ALLAHUMMA INNI A'OODHU BIKA MIN-AL-BUKHL WA A'OODHU BIKA MIN-AL JUBN, WA A'OODHU BIKA MIN AN NORADDA ILA ARDHALI AL OMR, WA A'OODHU BIKA MIN FITNATI DUNYA, WA 'ADHABI-L QABR.
O Allah! I seek refuge with You from miserliness, and seek refuge with You from cowardice, and seek refuge with You from being brought back to (senile) geriatric old age, and seek refuge with You from the affliction of the world and from the punishment in the Hereafter. (Bukhari)

ALLAHUMMA INNI AS'ALUKAL L-HUDA WATTUQA WAL 'AFAFA WAL GHINA.
O Allah! Indeed I, I ask of You, guidance, piety and chastity and to be free of depending upon anyone (except You). (Muslim)

ALLAHUMMA IGHFIRLI DHAMBI KULLAHU DIQQAHU WA JILLAHU WA AWWALAHU WA AKHIRAHU WA 'ALANIYATAHU WA SIRRAHU.
O Allah! Forgive all my sins, whether few or more, the first and the last, the apparent and the hidden. (Muslim)

YA MUSARRIFA-L QULOOBI SARRIF QALBI ALA TA'ATIK.
O Allah! The One Who turns the hearts, turn my heart towards Your obedience. (Muslim)

ALLAHUMM ANFA'NI BIMA 'ALLAMTANI WA 'ALLIMNI MA YANFA'NI WA ZIDNI 'ILMA.
O Allah! Benefit me through what You teach me and teach me what is beneficial for me and increase me in knowledge. (Ibn Majah)

ALLAHUMMA INNI A'UDHU BIKA MIN ZAWALI NI'MATIKA, WA TAHAWWULI 'AFIYATIKA, WA FUJA'ATI NIQMATIKA, WA JAMI'I SAKHATIKA.
O Allah! I seek refuge in You against the declining of Your Favours, passing of safety, the suddenness of Your punishment and all that which displeases You. (Muslim)

ALLAHUMMA INNI AS'ALUKA MUJIBATI RAHMATIKA, WA 'AZA'IMA MAGHFIRATIKA, WAS-SALAMATA MIN KULLI ITHMIN, WAL-GHANIMATA MIN KULLI BIRRIN, WAL-FAWZA BIL- JANNATI, WANNAJATA MINA-NAR.
O Allah! I beg You for that which incites Your Mercy and the means of Your forgiveness, safety from every sin, the benefit from every good deed, success in attaining Jannah and deliverance from Fire. (Al Hakim)

LA ILAHA ILLALLAHUL-AZIMUL-HALIM. LA ILAHA ILLALLAHU RABBUL-'ARSHIL-'AZIM. LA ILAHA ILLALLAHU RABBUS-SAMAWATI, WA RABBUL-ARDI, WA RABBUL-'ARSHIL- KARIM.
None has the right to be worshipped but Allah the Incomparably Great, the Compassionate. None has the right to be worshipped but Allah the Rubb of the Mighty Throne. None has the right to be worshipped but Allah the Rubb of the heavens, the Rubb of the earth, and the Rubb of the Honourable Throne. (Bukhari & Muslim)

Rabbana Du'as

A collection of 40 du'as from the qur'an, which have endless benefits and virtues in islam.

RABBANA TAQABBAL MINNA INNAKA ANTAS SAMEEAUL ALEEM
Our Lord! Accept (this service) from us: For Thou art the All-Hearing, the All-knowing [2:127]

RABBANA WA-J'ALNA MUSLIMAYNI LAKA MA MIN DHURRIYATINA 'UMMATAN MUSLIMATAN LAKA WA 'ARINA MANASIKANA WA TUB 'ALAYNA 'INNAKA 'ANTAT-TAWWABU-RAHEEM
Our Lord! Make of us Muslims, bowing to Thy (Will), and of our progeny a people Muslim, bowing to Thy (will); and show us our place for the celebration of (due) rites; and turn unto us (in Mercy); for Thou art the Oft-Returning, Most Merciful [2:128]

RABBANA ATINA FID-DUNYA HASANATAN WA FIL 'AKHIRATI HASANATAN WAQINA 'ADHABAN-NAR
Our Lord! Grant us good in this world and good in the hereafter, and save us from the chastisement of the fire [2:201]

RABBANA AFRIGH 'ALAYNA SABRAN WA THABBIT AQDAMANA WANSURNA 'ALAL-QAWMIL-KAFIRIN
Our Lord! Bestow on us endurance, make our foothold sure, and give us help against the disbelieving folk [2:250]

RABBANA LA TU'AKHIDHNA IN-NASINA AW AKHTA'NA
Our Lord! Condemn us not if we forget or fall into error [2:286]

RABBANA WALA TAHMIL ALAYNA ISRAN KAMA HAMALTAHU 'ALAL-LADHEENA MIN QABLINA
Our Lord! Lay not on us a burden Like that which Thou didst lay on those before us [2:286]

RABBANA WALA TUHAMMILNA MA LA TAQATA LANA BIHI WA'FU ANNA WAGHFIR LANA WAIRHAMNA ANTA MAWLANA FANSURNA 'ALAL-QAWMIL KAFIREEN
Our Lord! Lay not on us a burden greater than we have strength to bear. Blot out our sins, and grant us forgiveness. Have mercy on us. Thou art our Protector; Help us against those who stand against faith [2:286]

RABBANA LA TUZIGH QULOOBANA BA'DA IDH HADAYTANA WA HAB LANA MILLADUNKA RAHMAH INNAKA ANTAL WAHHAB
Our Lord! (they say), Let not our hearts deviate now after Thou hast guided us, but grant us mercy from Thine own Presence; for Thou art the Grantor of bounties without measure [3:8]

RABBANA INNAKA JAMI'UNNASI LI-YAWMIL LA RAYBA RI INNALLAHA LA YUKHLIFUL MI'AAD
Our Lord! Thou art He that will gather mankind Together against a day about which there is no doubt; for Allah never fails in His promise [3:9]

RABBANA INNANA AMANNA FAGHFIR LANA DHUNUUBANA WA QINNA 'ADHABAN-NAAR
Our Lord! We have indeed believed: forgive us, then, our sins, and save us from the agony of the Fire [3:16]

RABBANA AMANNA BIMA ANZALTA WATTABA 'NAR-RUSULA FAK-TUBNA MA'ASH-SHAHIDEEN
Our Lord! We believe in what Thou hast revealed, and we follow the Messenger. Then write us down among those who bear witness [3:53]

RABBANA-GHFIR LANA DHUNUUBANA WA ISRAFANA FI AMRINA WA THABBIT AQDAMANA WANSURNA 'ALAL QAWMIL KAFIREEN
Our Lord! Forgive us our sins and anything We may have done that transgressed our duty: Establish our feet firmly, and help us against those that resist Faith [3:147]

RABBANA MA KHALAQTA HADHA BATILA SUBHANAKA FAQINA 'ADHABAN-NAAR
Our Lord! Not for naught Hast Thou created (all) this! Glory to Thee! Give us salvation from the penalty of the Fire [3:191]

RABBANA INNAKA MAN TUDKHILIN NARA FAQAD AKHZAYTAH WA MA LIDH-DHALIMEENA MIN ANSAR
Our Lord! Any whom Thou dost admit to the Fire, Truly Thou coverest with shame, and never will wrong-doers Find any helpers! [3:192]

RABBANA INNANA SAMI'NA MUNADIYANY-YUNADI LIL-IMANI AN AMINU BI RABBIKUM FA'AAMANNA
Our Lord! We have heard the call of one calling (Us) to Faith, 'Believe ye in the Lord,' and we have believed [3:193]

RABBANA FAGHFIR LANA DHUNOOBANA WA KAFFIR 'ANA SAYYI'AATINA WA TAWAFFANA MA'AL ABRAR
Our Lord! Forgive us our sins, blot out from us our iniquities, and take to Thyself our souls in the company of the righteous [3:193]

RABBANA WA 'ATINA MA WA'ADTANA 'ALA RUSULIKA WA LA TUKHZINA YAWMAL-QIYAMAH INNAKA LA TUKHLIFUL MI'AAD
Our Lord! Grant us what Thou didst promise unto us through Thine apostles, and save us from shame on the Day of Judgment: For Thou never breakest Thy promise [3:194]

RABBANA AAMANA FAKTUBNA MA' ASH-SHAHIDEEN
Our Lord! We believe; write us down among the witnesses [5:83]

RABBANA ANZIL 'ALAYNA MA'IDATAM MINAS-SAMAI TUKNU LANA 'IDAL LI-AWWA-LINA WA AAKHIRNA WA AYATAM-MINKA WAR-ZUQNA WA ANTA KHAYRUL-RAZIQEEN
O Allah our Lord! Send us from heaven a table set (with viands), that there may be for us - for the first and the last of us - a solemn festival and a sign from thee; and provide for our sustenance, for thou art the best Sustainer (of our needs) [5:114]

RABBANA ZALAMNA ANFUSINA WA IL LAM TAGHFIR LANA WA TARHAMNA LANA KUNA MINAL-KHASIREEN
Our Lord! We have wronged our own souls: If thou forgive us not and bestow not upon us Thy Mercy, we shall certainly be lost [7:23]

RABBANA LA TAJ'ALNA MA'AL QAWWMI-DHALIMEEN
Our Lord! Send us not to the company of the wrong-doers [7:47]

RABBANA IFTAH BAYANA WABAYNA QAWMINA BIL HAQQI WA ANTA KHAYRUL ALFATIHEEN
Our Lord! Decide Thou between us and our people in truth, for Thou art the best to decide [7:89]

RABBANA AFRIGH 'ALAYNA SABRAW WA TAWAFFANA MUSLIMEEN
Our Lord! Pour out on us patience and constancy, and take our souls unto thee as Muslims (who bow to thy will)! [7:126]

RABBANA LA TAJ'ALNA FIRNATAL LIL-QAWMIDH-DHALIMEEN WA NAJJINA BI-RAHMATIKA MINAL QAWMIL KAFIREEN
Our Lord! Make us not a trial for those who practise oppression; And deliver us by Thy Mercy from those who reject (Thee) [10:85-86]

RABBANA INNAKA TA'IAMU MA NUKHFI WA MA NU'LIN WA MA YAKHFA 'ALAL-LAHI MIN SHAY'IN FIL-ARDI WA LA FIS-SAMA'
O our Lord! Truly Thou dost know what we conceal and what we reveal: for nothing whatever is hidden from Allah, whether on earth or in heaven [14:38]

RABBANA WA TAQABBAL DU'A
O our Lord! And accept my Prayer [14:40]

RABBANA GHFIR LI WA LI WALLIDAYYA WA LIL MU'MINEENA YAWMA YAQUMUL HISAAB
O our Lord! Cover (us) with Thy Forgiveness - me, my parents, and (all) Believers, on the Day that the Reckoning will be established! [14:41]

RABBANA 'ATINA MIL-LADUNKA RAHMATAW WA HAYYA LANA MIN AMRINA RASHADA
Our Lord! Bestow on us Mercy from Thyself, and dispose of our affair for us in the right way! [18:10]

RABBANA INNANA NAKHAFU ANY-YAFRUTA 'ALAYNA AW ANY-YATGHA
Our Lord! We fear lest he hasten with insolence against us, or lest he transgress all bounds [20: 45]

RABBANA AMANNA FAGHFIR LANA WARHAMNA WA ANTA KHAYRUR RAHIMIIN
Our Lord! We believe; then do Thou forgive us, and have mercy upon us: For Thou art the Best of those who show mercy [23: 109]

RABBANAS-RIF 'ANNA 'ADHABA JAHANNAMA INNA 'ADHABAHA KANA GHARAMA INNAHA SA'AT MUSTA-QARRANW WA MUQAMA
Our Lord! Avert from us the Wrath of Hell, for its Wrath is indeed an affliction grievous,- Evil indeed is it as an abode, and as a place to rest in [25: 65-66]

RABBANA HABLANA MIN AZWAAJINA WADHURRIY-YATINA, QURRATA 'AYIONI WA-JALNA LIL-MUTTAQEENA IMAAMA
O my Lord! Grant unto us wives and offspring who will be the comfort of our eyes, and give us (the grace) to lead the righteous [25:74]

RABBANA LA GHAFURUN SHAKUR
Our Lord is indeed Oft-Forgiving Ready to appreciate (service) [35: 34]

RABBANA WASI'TA KULLA SHA'IR RAHMATANW WA 'ILMAN FAGHFIR LILLADHINA TABU WATTABA'U SABILAKA WAQIHIM 'ADHABAL-JAHIIM
Our Lord! Thy Reach is over all things, in Mercy and Knowledge. Forgive, then, those who turn in Repentance, and follow Thy Path; and preserve them from the Penalty of the Blazing Fire! [40:7]

RABBANA WA ADHKHILUM JANNATI 'ADNINIL-LATI WA'ATTAHUM WA MAN SALAHA MIN ABA'IHIM WA AZAJIHIM WA DHURIYYATIHIM INNAKA ANTAL 'AZIZUL-HAKIM, WAQIHIMUS SAYYI'AT WA MAN TAQIS-SAYYI'ATI YAWMA'IDHIN FAQAD RAHIMATAHU WA DHALIKA HUWAL FAWZUL-'ADHEEM
And grant, our Lord! that they enter the Gardens of Eternity, which Thou hast promised to them, and to the righteous among their fathers, their wives, and their posterity! For Thou art (He), the Exalted in Might, Full of Wisdom. And preserve them from (all) ills; and any whom Thou dost preserve from ills that Day,- on them wilt Thou have bestowed Mercy indeed: and that will be truly (for them) the highest Achievement [40:8-9]

RABBANA-GHFIR LANA WA LI 'IKHWANI NALLADHINA SABAQUNA BIL IMANI WA LA TAJ'AL FI QULUBINA GHILLAL-LILLADHINA AMANU
Our Lord! Forgive us, and our brethren who came before us into the Faith, and leave not, in our hearts, rancour (or sense of injury) against those who have believed [59:10]

RABBANA INNAKA RA'UFUR RAHIM
Our Lord! Thou art indeed Full of Kindness, Most Merciful [59:10]

RABBANA 'ALAYKA TAWAKKALNA WA-ILAYKA ANABNA WA-ILAYKAL MASIR
Our Lord! In Thee do we trust, and to Thee do we turn in repentance: to Thee is (our) Final Goal [60:4]

RABBANA LA TAJ'ALNA FITNATAL LILLADHINA KAFARU WAGHFIR LANA RABBANA INNAKA ANTAL 'AZIZUL-HAKIM
Our Lord! Make us not a (test and) trial for the Unbelievers, but forgive us, our Lord! for Thou art the Exalted in Might, the Wise [60:5]

RABBANA ATMIM LANA NURANA WAIGHFIR LANA INNAKA 'ALA KULLI SHAY-IN QADIR
Our Lord! Perfect our Light for us, and grant us Forgiveness: for Thou hast power over all things [66:8]

Some Hadith About Ramadan

When the month of Ramadan starts, the gates of the heaven are opened and the gates of Hell are closed and the devils are chained.
Bukhari and Muslim

Abu Huraiyra ﷺ related that the Prophet ﷺ said: Whoever fasts during Ramadan with faith and seeking his reward from Allah will have his past sins forgiven. Whoever prays during the nights in Ramadan with faith and seeking his reward from Allah will have his past sins forgiven. And he who passes Laylat-ul-Qadr in prayer with faith and seeking his reward from Allah will have his past sins forgiven.
Bukhari and Muslim

Abu Huraiyra ﷺ related that the Prophet ﷺ said: If anyone omits his fast even for one day in Ramadan without a concession or without being ill, then if he were to fast for the rest of his life he could not make up for it.
Bukhari

Abu Huraiyra ﷺ related that the Prophet ﷺ said: Allah the Majestic and Exalted said, "Every deed of man will receive 10 to 700 times reward, except *Siyam* (fasting), for it is for Me and I shall reward it (as I like). There are two occasions of joy for one who fasts: one when he breaks the fast and the other when he will meet his Lord."
Muslim

Anas ﷺ related that the Prophet ﷺ said: Take the Suhoor meal, for there is blessing in it.
Bukhari and Muslim

Salman ibn Amir Dhabi ؓ related that the Prophet ﷺ said: Break your fast with dates, or else with water, for it is pure.
Abu Dawud and Tirmidhi

Abu Huraiyra ؓ related that the Prophet ﷺ said: If anyone forgets that he is fasting and eats or drinks he should complete his fast, for it is Allah who has fed him and given him drink.
Bukhari and Muslim

Zaid ibn Khalid Juhni ؓ related that the Prophet ﷺ said: He who provides for the breaking of the fast of another person earns the same merit as the one who was fasting, without diminishing in any way the reward of the latter.
Tirmidhi

The Qur'an

'Aisha ؓ relates that the Prophet ﷺ said: Verily the one who recites the Qur'an beautifully, smoothly, and precisely, he will be in the company of the noble and obedient angels. And as for the one who recites with difficulty, stammering or stumbling through its verses, then he will have twice that reward.

Bukhari and Muslim

Ramadan is the month of the Qur'an, so make as much time as you can this month to make it your main focus. Set aside fixed times each day, perhaps after each salah, or an hour before Maghrib, to recite the Qur'an. No matter what your skill level is at with reciting, praying often will help make you more fluent.

Write down your Qur'an goals here:

....
....
....
....
....
....
....
....
....
....
....
....
....
....

Qur'an Juz Checklist:

1 ☐	6 ☐	11 ☐	16 ☐	21 ☐	26 ☐
2 ☐	7 ☐	12 ☐	17 ☐	22 ☐	27 ☐
3 ☐	8 ☐	13 ☐	18 ☐	23 ☐	28 ☐
4 ☐	9 ☐	14 ☐	19 ☐	24 ☐	29 ☐
5 ☐	10 ☐	15 ☐	20 ☐	25 ☐	30 ☐

Du'as

Write down a list of your du'as for this month. Don't forget to include your family, friends, and people that you know who have specific problems - and of course the ummah around the world.

Sadaqah and Zakah

Did you know that sadaqah comes in many forms, and not just giving money in charity?

This includes helping your parents with chores around the house or preparing iftaar, being kind to a neighbour (Muslim or Non-Muslim, it doesn't matter), and being nice to your younger siblings.

"[O Muhammad], tell My servants who have believed to establish prayer and spend from what We have provided them, secretly and publicly, before a Day comes in which there will be no exchange, nor any friendships."

Ibrahim: 31

You can of course donate to charity, and remember that if you have reached the age of puberty and if you have savings, you must pay Zakah

Zakah is one of the five pillars of Islam and is compulsory for all Muslims. Each year a payment must be made, worth 2.5% of your savings, and this cleanses your money and possessions by teaching you not to place too much value on material wealth.

By paying Zakah, we are given the opportunity to share our excess wealth with those less fortunate than ourselves. Remember, we and our wealth belong to Allah - He is the real owner and we are simply the trustees of His wealth. Through paying Zakah, we fulfil our duty as trustees.

These are some recommended charities to whom you can give your Zakah:
Islamic Relief: www.islamic-relief.com/uk
Ummah Welfare Trust: www.uwt.org
Muslim Hands: muslimhands.org.uk

Or visit www.launchGood.com to choose from the hundreds of charitable campaigns featured.

Write down your Zakah and Sadaqah plans here:

Using Your Time Wisely

Abu Huraiyra ؓ related that the Prophet ﷺ said: If a person does not avoid false talk and false conduct during Siyam (fasting), then Allah does not care if he abstains from food and drink.

Bukhari, Muslim

Try not to spend your days sleeping and killing time on social media, but use your time productively to gain as much reward as you can.

There's no harm in connecting with friends, but an occasional social media fast is always a good thing to try to put into practice, so try to pull back as much as you can.

It may help to plan a daily timetable, where you can fit in your homework and Qur'an around school. Definitely include naps, as you will be tired from Tarawih and waking for suhoor. A nap during the day, or after school, can help keep you going until late.

Write down your throughts on how you can be most productive. Include Salaah, Qur'an, homework, school and naps.

....
....
....
....
....
....
....
....
....
....

Laylat-ul-Qadr

This is the Night of Power. It is one of the nights of the last ten days of Ramadan, and on this night the blessings and mercy of Allah ﷻ are abundant, sins are forgiven and du'as are accepted.

"Verily! We have sent it (this Quran) down in the night of Al-Qadr.
And what will make you know what the night of Al-Qadr is?
The night of Al-Qadr is better than a thousand months
Therein descend the angels and the Ruh (Gabriel) by Allah's Permission with all Decrees,
Peace! until the appearance of dawn."

Qur'an: 97:1-5

'Aisha ؓ related that the Prophet ﷺ said: Look for Laylat-ul-Qadr on an odd-numbered night during the last ten nights of Ramadan.

Bukhari

Anas ibn Malik ؓ related that the Prophet ﷺ said: When Laylat-ul-Qadr comes Gabriel descends with a company of angels who ask for blessings on everyone who is remembering Allah, whether they are sitting or standing.

Baihaqi

Laylat-ul-Qadr Tips

Prepare your list of the specific du'as you want to make, be extra thorough. Be sure to include this du'a:
'Aisha ؓ reported: I asked: "O Messenger of Allah! If I realise Laylat-ul-Qadr (Night of Decree), what should I supplicate in it?" He replied, "You should supplicate:
ALLAHUMMA INNAKA 'AFUWWUN, TUHIBBUL-'AFWA, FA'FU 'ANNI
(O Allah, You are Most Forgiving, and You love forgiveness; so forgive me)."
At-Tirmidhi

Read Surah Al-Qadr along with its Tafseer (listen to one on an app or watch one on YouTube) for a deeper understanding and connection to this incredible night.

Eat light but well and remain hydrated so that you can fully participate in these days.

Complete as much of your 'Eid prep as possible before these blessed days begin.

Leave extra time for your prayers so that you may reflect more and offer more du'a.

Of course you don't have to pray Tarawih in the masjid, but you should still pray it at home. You won't ever regret it if you do!

Spend every possible moment making du'a and dhikr.

The Great 'Eid Plan

Plan your 'Eid as early as possible so that it's not taking over your time during the last 10 days of Ramadan.

Write down your ideas here on how to make it the best 'Eid yet:

Shopping list (clothes and gifts):

Your ideal menu:

DAY 1

Suhoor time: *Iftaar time:*

Salah:

☐ Fajr   ☐ Dhuhr   ☐ 'Asr   ☐ Maghrib   ☐ 'Isha

Qur'an: *How much have you recited? Did you meet today's goals?*

Reflect: *How was your day?*

Water: *Be sure to drink as much water as you can between iftaar and suhoor.*

DAY 2

Suhoor time: Iftaar time:

Salah:

☐ Fajr   ☐ Dhuhr   ☐ 'Asr   ☐ Maghrib   ☐ 'Isha

Qur'an: *How much have you recited? Did you meet today's goals?*

Reflect: *How was your day?*

Water: *Be sure to drink as much water as you can between iftaar and suhoor.*

1 2 3 4 5 6 7 8

DAY 3

Suhoor time: Iftaar time:

Salah:

☐ Fajr   ☐ Dhuhr   ☐ 'Asr   ☐ Maghrib   ☐ 'Isha

Qur'an: *How much have you recited? Did you meet today's goals?*

Reflect: *How was your day?*

Water: *Be sure to drink as much water as you can between iftaar and suhoor.*

DAY 4

Suhoor time: Iftaar time:

Salah:

☐ Fajr   ☐ Dhuhr   ☐ 'Asr   ☐ Maghrib   ☐ 'Isha

Qur'an: *How much have you recited? Did you meet today's goals?*

Reflect: *How was your day?*

Water: *Be sure to drink as much water as you can between iftaar and suhoor.*

DAY 5

Suhoor time: Iftaar time:

Salah:
☐ Fajr   ☐ Dhuhr   ☐ 'Asr   ☐ Maghrib   ☐ 'Isha

Qur'an: *How much have you recited? Did you meet today's goals?*

Reflect: *How was your day?*

Water: *Be sure to drink as much water as you can between iftaar and suhoor.*

DAY 6

Suhoor time: *Iftaar time:*

Salah:

☐ Fajr ☐ Dhuhr ☐ 'Asr ☐ Maghrib ☐ 'Isha

Qur'an: *How much have you recited? Did you meet today's goals?*

Reflect: *How was your day?*

Water: *Be sure to drink as much water as you can between iftaar and suhoor.*

DAY 7

Suhoor time: *Iftaar time:*

Salah:

☐ Fajr   ☐ Dhuhr   ☐ 'Asr   ☐ Maghrib   ☐ 'Isha

Qur'an: *How much have you recited? Did you meet today's goals?*

Reflect: *How was your day?*

Water: *Be sure to drink as much water as you can between iftaar and suhoor.*

DAY 8

Suhoor time: Iftaar time:

Salah:

☐ Fajr   ☐ Dhuhr   ☐ 'Asr   ☐ Maghrib   ☐ 'Isha

Qur'an: *How much have you recited? Did you meet today's goals?*

Reflect: *How was your day?*

Water: *Be sure to drink as much water as you can between iftaar and suhoor.*

DAY 9

Suhoor time: Iftaar time:

Salah:

- [ ] Fajr - [ ] Dhuhr - [ ] 'Asr - [ ] Maghrib - [ ] 'Isha

Qur'an: *How much have you recited? Did you meet today's goals?*

Reflect: *How was your day?*

Water: *Be sure to drink as much water as you can between iftaar and suhoor.*

DAY 10

Suhoor time: Iftaar time:

Salah:

☐ Fajr ☐ Dhuhr ☐ 'Asr ☐ Maghrib ☐ 'Isha

Qur'an: *How much have you recited? Did you meet today's goals?*

Reflect: *How was your day?*

Water: *Be sure to drink as much water as you can between iftaar and suhoor.*

DAY 11

Suhoor time:　　　　*Iftaar time:*

Salah:
- [ ] Fajr　　[ ] Dhuhr　　[ ] 'Asr　　[ ] Maghrib　　[ ] 'Isha

Qur'an: *How much have you recited? Did you meet today's goals?*

Reflect: *How was your day?*

Water: *Be sure to drink as much water as you can between iftaar and suhoor.*

DAY 12

Suhoor time: Iftaar time:

Salah:

☐ Fajr   ☐ Dhuhr   ☐ 'Asr   ☐ Maghrib   ☐ 'Isha

Qur'an: *How much have you recited? Did you meet today's goals?*

Reflect: *How was your day?*

Water: *Be sure to drink as much water as you can between iftaar and suhoor.*

1 2 3 4 5 6 7 8

DAY 13

Suhoor time: Iftaar time:

Salah:

☐ Fajr   ☐ Dhuhr   ☐ 'Asr   ☐ Maghrib   ☐ 'Isha

Qur'an: *How much have you recited? Did you meet today's goals?*

Reflect: *How was your day?*

Water: *Be sure to drink as much water as you can between iftaar and suhoor.*

DAY 14

Suhoor time: Iftaar time:

Salah:

- [ ] Fajr - [ ] Dhuhr - [ ] 'Asr - [ ] Maghrib - [ ] 'Isha

Qur'an: *How much have you recited? Did you meet today's goals?*

Reflect: *How was your day?*

Water: *Be sure to drink as much water as you can between iftaar and suhoor.*

DAY 15

Suhoor time:　　　　Iftaar time:

Salah:
- [ ] Fajr　　[ ] Dhuhr　　[ ] 'Asr　　[ ] Maghrib　　[ ] 'Isha

Qur'an: *How much have you recited? Did you meet today's goals?*

Reflect: *How was your day?*

Water: *Be sure to drink as much water as you can between iftaar and suhoor.*

DAY 16

Suhoor time: *Iftaar time:*

Salah:

☐ Fajr   ☐ Dhuhr   ☐ 'Asr   ☐ Maghrib   ☐ 'Isha

Qur'an: *How much have you recited? Did you meet today's goals?*

Reflect: *How was your day?*

Water: *Be sure to drink as much water as you can between iftaar and suhoor.*

DAY 17

Suhoor time: Iftaar time:

Salah:
☐ Fajr   ☐ Dhuhr   ☐ 'Asr   ☐ Maghrib   ☐ 'Isha

Qur'an: *How much have you recited? Did you meet today's goals?*

Reflect: *How was your day?*

Water: *Be sure to drink as much water as you can between iftaar and suhoor.*

DAY 18

Suhoor time: Iftaar time:

Salah:

☐ Fajr   ☐ Dhuhr   ☐ 'Asr   ☐ Maghrib   ☐ 'Isha

Qur'an: *How much have you recited? Did you meet today's goals?*

Reflect: *How was your day?*

Water: *Be sure to drink as much water as you can between iftaar and suhoor.*

DAY 19

Suhoor time: Iftaar time:

Salah:

☐ Fajr   ☐ Dhuhr   ☐ 'Asr   ☐ Maghrib   ☐ 'Isha

Qur'an: *How much have you recited? Did you meet today's goals?*

Reflect: *How was your day?*

Water: *Be sure to drink as much water as you can between iftaar and suhoor.*

DAY 20

Suhoor time: *Iftaar time:*

Sa'ah:
- [ ] Fajr [ ] Dhuhr [ ] 'Asr [ ] Maghrib [ ] 'Isha

Qur'an: *How much have you recited? Did you meet today's goals?*

Reflect: *How was your day?*

Water: *Be sure to drink as much water as you can between iftaar and suhoor.*

DAY 21

Suhoor time: Iftaar time:

Salah:

☐ Fajr   ☐ Dhuhr   ☐ 'Asr   ☐ Maghrib   ☐ 'Isha

Qur'an: *How much have you recited? Did you meet today's goals?*

Reflect: *How was your day?*

Water: *Be sure to drink as much water as you can between iftaar and suhoor.*

DAY 22

Suhoor time: Iftaar time:

Salah:
- [ ] Fajr
- [ ] Dhuhr
- [ ] 'Asr
- [ ] Maghrib
- [ ] 'Isha

Qur'an: *How much have you recited? Did you meet today's goals?*

Reflect: *How was your day?*

Water: *Be sure to drink as much water as you can between iftaar and suhoor.*

DAY 23

Suhoor time: Iftaar time:

Salah:
- ☐ Fajr ☐ Dhuhr ☐ 'Asr ☐ Maghrib ☐ 'Isha

Qur'an: *How much have you recited? Did you meet today's goals?*

Reflect: *How was your day?*

Water: *Be sure to drink as much water as you can between iftaar and suhoor.*

DAY 24

Suhoor time: Iftaar time:

Salah:

☐ Fajr   ☐ Dhuhr   ☐ 'Asr   ☐ Maghrib   ☐ 'Isha

Qur'an: *How much have you recited? Did you meet today's goals?*

Reflect: *How was your day?*

Water: *Be sure to drink as much water as you can between iftaar and suhoor.*

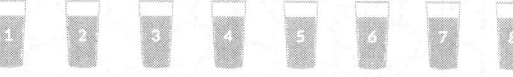

DAY 25

Suhoor time: Iftaar time:

Salah:

☐ Fajr   ☐ Dhuhr   ☐ 'Asr   ☐ Maghrib   ☐ 'Isha

Qur'an: *How much have you recited? Did you meet today's goals?*

Reflect: *How was your day?*

Water: *Be sure to drink as much water as you can between iftaar and suhoor.*

DAY 26

Suhoor time: *Iftaar time:*

Salah:

☐ Fajr   ☐ Dhuhr   ☐ 'Asr   ☐ Maghrib   ☐ 'Isha

Qur'an: *How much have you recited? Did you meet today's goals?*

Reflect: *How was your day?*

Water: *Be sure to drink as much water as you can between iftaar and suhoor.*

DAY 27

Suhoor time: Iftaar time:

Salah:
- [ ] Fajr [ ] Dhuhr [ ] 'Asr [ ] Maghrib [ ] 'Isha

Qur'an: *How much have you recited? Did you meet today's goals?*

Reflect: *How was your day?*

Water: *Be sure to drink as much water as you can between iftaar and suhoor.*

DAY 28

Suhoor time: *Iftaar time:*

Salah:

- [ ] Fajr
- [ ] Dhuhr
- [ ] 'Asr
- [ ] Maghrib
- [ ] 'Isha

Qur'an: *How much have you recited? Did you meet today's goals?*

Reflect: *How was your day?*

Water: *Be sure to drink as much water as you can between iftaar and suhoor.*

DAY 29

Suhoor time: Iftaar time:

Salah:

☐ Fajr   ☐ Dhuhr   ☐ 'Asr   ☐ Maghrib   ☐ 'Isha

Qur'an: *How much have you recited? Did you meet today's goals?*

Reflect: *How was your day?*

Water: *Be sure to drink as much water as you can between iftaar and suhoor.*

DAY 30

Suhoor time: Iftaar time:

Salah:

☐ Fajr   ☐ Dhuhr   ☐ 'Asr   ☐ Maghrib   ☐ 'Isha

Qur'an: *How much have you recited? Did you meet today's goals?*

Reflect: *How was your day?*

Water: *Be sure to drink as much water as you can between iftaar and suhoor.*

1   2   3   4   5   6   7   8

Taqabbal Allah minna wa minkum.
Wishing you and your loved ones a fabulous 'Eid.

Use the next couple of pages to write about your 'Eid, or reflect on your Ramadan. What would you do to make your Ramadan better next year?

www.reyoflightdesign.com/store

All rights reserved. No part of this publication may be reproduced in any language, stored in any retrieval system or transmitted in any form or by any means - electronic, mechanical, photocopying, recording or otherwise - without the express permission of the copyright owner.

Printed in Great Britain
by Amazon